A
HISTORY
OF *Television*

ESSENTIAL LIBRARY OF CULTURAL HISTORY

A HISTORY OF *Television*

by M. M. Eboch

Content Consultant
Karen Petruska, PhD
Media Industries Project
University of California, Santa Barbara

An Imprint of Abdo Publishing | www.abdopublishing.com

www.abdopublishing.com

Published by Abdo Publishing, a division of ABDO, PO Box 398166, Minneapolis, Minnesota 55439. Copyright © 2015 by Abdo Consulting Group, Inc. International copyrights reserved in all countries. No part of this book may be reproduced in any form without written permission from the publisher. Essential Library™ is a trademark and logo of Abdo Publishing.

Printed in the United States of America, North Mankato, Minnesota
102014
012015

Cover Photo: Shutterstock Images
Interior Photos: AP Images, 1 (left), 1 (right), 47, 55, 100; Kobby Dagan/Shutterstock Images, 3 (top), 82; Peter "Hopper" Stone/ABC/AP Images, 3 (bottom), 91; Dragon Images/Shutterstock Images, 7; Twin Design/Shutterstock Images, 10, 101; iStockphoto, 12–13; Everett Collection/Shutterstock Images, 14; Bettmann/Corbis, 20, 24, 35, 38, 62, 65, 77, 98; akg-images/Newscom, 23; The Firestone Company News Bureau, 27, 99; Red Line Editorial, 33, 97; Evert F. Baumgardner, 36; CBS-TV/Album/Newscom, 40; Radio Corporation of America, 50; Brad Camembert/Shutterstock Images, 57; Heritage Images/ Glow Images, 59; Everett Collection/Newscom, 67; Album/Newscom, 73; Shutterstock Images, 79; Handout/MCT/Newscom, 81

Editor: Jenna Gleisner
Series Designer: Maggie Villaume

Library of Congress Control Number: 2014943867

Cataloging-in-Publication Data

Eboch, M.M.
A history of television / M.M. Eboch.
    p. cm. -- (Essential library of cultural history)
ISBN 978-1-62403-556-2 (lib. bdg.)
Includes bibliographical references and index.
1. Television--History--Juvenile literature.   I. Title.
384--dc23

                                                    2014943867

CONTENTS

Chapter 1

Television Connects Cultures

In a discussion of art and culture, television may not immediately spring to mind. Yet, television has a broad cultural influence. On average, Americans spend more than 20 hours each week watching television.[1] In contrast, few people visit a museum or attend a concert every week. For decades, television has been a major part of people's lives. This has allowed the medium to influence both individual and national identities. Millions of people, spread thousands of miles apart, share the same experiences through television.

Television as an art form is dependent on the art forms that came before it. Television is a direct descendent of radio, in terms of both the technology

Television brings families and cultures together through shared experiences.

used and the content presented. Many of the program genres popular today, from soap operas to detective stories to family comedies, started with radio. Movies also influenced how stories are told and the visual tools used to tell them. Even politics have played a part, with government funding and regulations controlling how the television industry grew.

In the early days of television, it was viewed as a savior of culture. It would make society better by teaching people about the world and bringing quality entertainment directly into family homes. A few years later, the true nature of television became clear. It was primarily a way to provide mainstream

How Much Television?

Although children and teenagers are often accused of watching too much television, viewing rates are actually dropping among young adults. In addition, statistics show older adults watch more television than teenagers. Nielsen, a company that measures television audiences, reported in 2014 that Americans aged 18 to 24 were watching slightly less than 22 hours of traditional television each week. This continued a downward trend, dropping approximately 4.5 hours compared to three years before. It is possible teenagers and young adults who are watching less television are watching DVDs or playing video games instead. In contrast, television watching increased among people age 50 and older. Those above age 65 spend an average of almost 48 hours watching television each week.[2]

entertainment and sell products for the advertisers who paid for the shows. Still, television developed as a cultural art form, experimenting with new genres, new storytelling techniques, and new ways to entertain. Television also educates the public, exploring issues through fiction and nonfiction programs and bringing news from around the world. This helps reveal the full diversity of our world.

Soap operas got their name because they were often sponsored by the manufacturers of household cleaning products.

Combining Cultures

Television is an example of the way technology and society intertwine. For example, television news does not always cover the most important nationwide events. Instead, it may focus on the most visual. In 1949, three-year-old Kathy Fiscus fell into a well in Los Angeles, California. A local television station joined the print and radio reporters covering the story. Rescue efforts lasted more than 50 hours, and more than half of those were shown live on television. People gathered around television sets in store windows and at neighbors'

Thanks to apps such as Netflix, viewers can now experience television and movies on the go.

homes to watch the story unfold. At the same time, another girl drowned in a fishpond at home. Yet, few people followed her story. It had little effect, because it didn't play out on television. Today, decades later, our understanding of the world is filtered through what plays well on television.

In the beginning, television brought people together through shared entertainment. Because people had few choices of what to watch, they could expect their neighbors, classmates, and coworkers had seen the same shows. Over the years, new systems of distribution developed, from cable to satellite to the Internet. This allows access to many more stations and a much greater variety of programming. This diversity has helped people find small communities of shared interests.

In response to the changing technology, television programming changed, both reflecting and influencing culture. New methods of watching television also arose, with viewers moving away from the traditional television set and watching shows on computers and phones. This is changing the very definition of what it means to watch television.

THE FACE OF TELEVISION TODAY

Fifty years ago, watching television meant sitting in front of a television set and watching programs provided by the three networks: National Broadcasting Company (NBC), American Broadcasting Company (ABC), and Columbia Broadcasting System (CBS). Then cable, and later satellite, offered more choices from new networks and cable stations. Today, televisions are also used for watching DVDs and playing video games. Streaming on-demand companies, such as Netflix and Hulu, can be watched on a television set, a computer, or a phone.

The history of television has had a wide impact, both positive and negative, particularly on the United States and US culture throughout the last century.

Chapter 2

Radio with Pictures

*A*ncient methods of long-distance communication suffered major limitations. Smoke signals and drumbeats had a limited range. Letters took weeks or months to travel long distances. These delays had dramatic effects on people's lives. For example, President Abraham Lincoln delivered the Emancipation Proclamation, which freed slaves, on January 1, 1863. The news did not reach the state of Texas until June 19, 1865—a full two and a half years later. During that time, slaves in Texas continued to live in slavery because they did not know they were free. Many technologies have bridged the gap between ancient and modern communications.

Years before television brought news to the corners of the world, telegraphs were used to communicate.

A woman uses a telegraph to send Morse code.

Television is a relatively recent and highly important technology that has helped connect cultures.

New means of long-distance communication appeared in the 1800s. The first telegraph message was sent in 1844. The telegraph transmitted electric signals through a wire laid between two stations. Messages were sent as a series of dots and dashes called Morse code. For the first time ever, two people in distant cities could communicate in a matter of seconds.

The telegraph system quickly expanded. By 1866, a telegraph line spanned the Atlantic Ocean, connecting the United States and Europe. International news could be exchanged immediately. This changed many aspects of life. It even changed how wars were fought and likely affected who won. Journalists reported back to their newspapers quickly, so events were covered right away.

Radio Technology

At first, the telegraph only worked along wires, so it could not transmit information to any city without a connected telegraph station. Wireless telegraphs solved this problem beginning in 1891. The wireless telegraph could send coded messages through the air without connecting wires. An antenna sent a signal that another antenna picked up. Wireless telegraphs sent signals using radio waves. Today, radio waves are used in many technologies, including radio and television broadcasting, mobile phones, satellites, and wireless systems.

EINSTEIN'S TAKE ON RADIO

World-renowned physicist Albert Einstein was asked to explain radio in 1938, and he responded, "You see, wire telegraph is a kind of a very, very long cat. You pull his tail in New York and his head is meowing in Los Angeles. Do you understand this? And radio operates exactly the same way: you send signals here, they receive them there. The only difference is that there is no cat."[1]

Early radio technology led to broadcast radio, a business still in place today. The first program of speech and music was transmitted to the public in 1906. As inventors improved radio, public demand grew. The first commercial radio stations opened in 1920. Within a decade, millions of Americans were regularly listening to the radio. Programs included dramas, comedies, music, variety shows, and game shows.

Visual Radio

Some inventors were already at work on the next big thing. If radio could transmit sound, why couldn't a device transmit pictures as well? Several people contributed to the invention of a television set. In the 1920s, Scottish engineer John Logie Baird was at work in England, while American Charles Francis Jenkins worked in the United States. They each explored a mechanical television system using moving parts. A system of rotating disks produced flickering pictures for broadcast. The screens receiving the pictures were only approximately one inch (3 cm) wide, and the picture quality was poor. Yet, people were fascinated. Thousands of people built homemade television sets in an attempt to pick up these pictures.

On January 27, 1926, the first television was demonstrated in the United Kingdom. Baird had made progress with the mechanical system using spinning disks. He was able to transmit images in light and shadow, but they were barely visible.

In the United Kingdom, regularly scheduled television programming began in 1929. At first, the British Broadcasting Corporation (BBC) transmitted a picture after regular radio broadcasting was finished for the day. By March 1930, sound and pictures were transmitted together. In the United States, television was broadcast from approximately 25 stations by 1931.[2] The signals could travel hundreds of miles, so people did not have to live close to a station to view a television broadcast. Manufacturers sold television sets and kits to build them. However, because of the poor quality, mechanical television was destined to fail.

JUST FACES AND HANDS

The first television program to air in the United States was *The Queen's Messenger,* a suspense program about a diplomat and a mysterious woman. It aired live in September 1928 from Schenectady, New York. The system had many technical limitations. Because the screens on the mechanical televisions of the time were so small, only one actor's face or hands could be shown at a time. Two cameras focused on the actors. A third covered stage props and assistant actors showing their hands in gestures. The director watched through a television receiver and cut between cameras.

In the 1920s, the first years of broadcast radio, hundreds of companies and individuals set up their own radio stations. Reaching a large audience was important for satisfying advertisers. Therefore, stations tried to take over the best frequencies. The resulting chaos led the industry to ask the government for help. In 1927, Congress established the Federal Radio Commission (FRC) to regulate the airwaves in the United States. Station owners still wanted to buy specific frequencies. However, the FRC issued licenses for temporary use only. When a station applied for renewal, the FRC could judge whether it had served the "public interest, convenience, and necessity."[3] This forced radio stations to consider the public good as well as their own profits. The Federal Communications Commission (FCC) replaced the FRC in 1934.

Teen Television Genius

Philo T. Farnsworth was fascinated by technology of all types. When he was just 14 years old, he imagined a device that would divide a picture into lines of light and shade. The picture would be scanned and transmitted through the airwaves as electric pulses. An antenna would pick up the electric pulses. A receiver would then convert the pulses back into a series of lines, creating a picture on a television screen. Farnsworth believed this method, which used electricity rather than moving parts, would make better television transmissions.

Farnsworth was not the only inventor who saw the advantages of electricity. A Russian immigrant in New York was already working on an electronic television. Vladimir K. Zworykin was working at a manufacturing company. He demonstrated this television in the 1920s, but it was not well received.

In 1925, Farnsworth persuaded two California businessmen to invest $6,000 so he could build a television prototype. Farnsworth and his wife, Pem, moved to Hollywood, California, to work on the invention. They had to build a camera to turn an image into a stream of electrons. They also had to build a television tube to turn the stream of electrons back into a picture. Everything had to be made from scratch.

On September 7, 1927, Farnsworth demonstrated the electronic transmission of television to his financial backers. The first picture was merely a straight line. Later, he transmitted a dollar sign, intended to reassure his backers they would make money from his invention.

Farnsworth's wife, Pem, said of Philo, "He could foretell just what television was going to do for the world. It would make the world a smaller place, because we could watch what other people's lives were like, and they, in turn, could watch us."[4]

Farnsworth with his television receiver in 1930

The image was only the size of a postage stamp. Still, it was a major breakthrough.

Building these inventions cost money. Big companies became important financial backers. The Radio Corporation of America (RCA) controlled everything from the broadcast studios to the companies producing the radios. RCA was determined to be at the forefront of television.

Farnsworth received his first patent for television in 1930. RCA did not want to have to pay royalties on the technology. They offered Farnsworth $100,000 for his patents and business, but Farnsworth wanted control and a royalty. Years of legal battles followed, but there was a rush to develop the technology anyway. Farnsworth won a lawsuit against RCA, and the company had to pay him royalties. However, the Great Depression (1929–1939) and World War II (1939–1945) delayed the success of television.

A Crash Stops Progress

The development of television suffered a setback from the Wall Street financial crash in October 1929. Many companies went out of business. Most of the financial backing for new technology disappeared. Many television stations could not afford to update their equipment to the emerging electronic television system, so they went off the air. This gave temporary new life to radio, the cheapest source of entertainment. Soap operas, situation comedies, and singers were popular on radio. The biggest US radio broadcasters, NBC and CBS, used their radio income to advance their television operations. However, television did not really recover until the late 1930s.

Rise and Fall and Rise Again

$\mathcal{I}$n the 1930s, several companies produced television sets. Each brand could receive broadcasts only from its own local television station. The television was fun and fascinating but not practical for wide use. Sets were expensive, shows were broadcast for only a few hours a week, and reception was limited to local areas.

As the US economy recovered from the Great Depression in the late 1930s, incomes rose. RCA devoted $50 million to developing a fully electronic television system. It introduced this system in 1936 and spent several years doing test broadcasts.

By early 1939, the US economy was improving. RCA was determined to promote the sale of television sets.

Television sets of the 1930s were very expensive
and had small screens.

RCA president David Sarnoff speaks on television at the 1939 New York World's Fair.

That meant offering a regular broadcast. NBC, which was part of RCA, debuted this television service at the 1939 New York World's Fair. Only one camera covered the fair's opening event. Yet, this was a breakthrough moment. Thousands of people visited the NBC van at the fair and watched themselves on television.

RCA's president David Sarnoff called television "a new art so important in its implications that it is bound to affect all society. It is an art which shines like a torch of hope in a troubled world."[1] The New York World's Fair demonstration became known as the birth of television. The day after the fair opened, electronic television sets went on sale in the United States. People could choose from 25 models, ranging in price from $200 to $1,000. These televisions were standardized, so they could receive programming from any television station.

CBS also began adding television programming to its radio programming. Although popular, television demand did not meet the industry's hopes, and high prices were to blame. In 1939, the average US yearly income was $1,368, making even the cheapest television set out of reach for most families.[2] Fewer than 1,000 television sets were sold in New York in the first six months they were available. In early 1941, there were fewer than 3,000 television sets in New York City, among a population of more than 7 million.[3] No more than ten television stations were on the air across the country.

The FCC offered a theory. People would probably not

President Franklin D. Roosevelt delivered an opening address at the New York World's Fair in 1939, becoming the first president to appear on television.

COLOR TECHNOLOGY

In 1940, RCA and CBS each proposed new color television systems. But the color quality was poor, and current black-and-white sets would not pick up the signal. People had to buy new sets designed for color. The first color sets were sold in 1954. Each had a 15-inch (38 cm) screen and cost more than $1,000. Soon 19-inch (48 cm) and 21-inch (53 cm) sets were available, and prices dropped somewhat. Yet, prices were high, sets were unreliable, and few shows were broadcast in color. Color television set sales remained low until these problems were resolved in the mid-1960s.

buy television sets until there were more stations and better programs. In addition, televisions only showed black-and-white images. Color would probably be more appealing, but the technology was not available.

Commercial Television

How would the stations make money to pay for more programming? Television had been purely experimental up to that point as companies explored the technology. Television was paid for by the profits from radio. In May 1941, the FCC approved commercial television. This meant advertisers could sponsor a program so television could earn money directly. The first rates were $60 for an hour-long program during the day and $120 for an hour-long program in the evening. A sponsor's advertisement would play during the program. The first commercial was simply an image of a ticking watch with the sponsor's name, Bulova.

Television stations looked for inexpensive programs able to provide visual interest with limited technology. They studied what worked well on radio, but not every radio show translated well to images. Suspense and thriller programs could use spooky sound effects to create tension on the radio. The technology to do the same with visual effects either did not exist or was too expensive. Quiz and game shows worked well in a visual format. Simple camerawork could show the excited contestants. These programs introduced a format that would become a television standard for decades.

A woman poses with a faucet aerator in a 1948 commercial.

Reaching America

Just when television seemed ready to take on the world, war interfered. When the United States entered World War II in December 1941, the military needed television technology for radar and defense research. Companies were expected to contribute to the war effort, so commercial television was greatly reduced. Only eight US cities had commercial television service during the war.[4] The network stations in New York broadcast only one night a week. Home televisions were no longer manufactured, although hospitals used some to entertain wounded servicemen with the limited broadcasts.

When war seemed to be drawing to an end in 1943, the networks began expanding their programming. In New York City, shows broadcast every night of the week, though only from one network each night. People who wanted to watch a television program had one option.

In 1948, CBS introduced the *CBS Television News*. This 15-minute show covered the headlines using newsreel film, or filmed documentaries. CBS also began producing new entertainment shows, usually based on popular radio shows. Yet, CBS still believed television was in the experimental stage. It hoped color technology could progress before the industry expanded.

Advertisers were already becoming more interested in the new medium, however. The head of a large radio advertising firm produced a show for television. "The Peanut Is a Serious Guy" was a 15-minute advertisement for peanuts.

In 1945, NBC split into two companies. One retained the NBC name, and the other became the American Broadcasting Company (ABC). ABC became the fourth major network, alongside CBS, NBC, and DuMont Television Network, which went out of business in 1955. In the three years after the war, the number of commercial television stations grew from nine to 48.[5]

Entertaining America

Early television stations transmitted a limited distance. Each station produced its own shows, which

AMERICA'S FAVORITE UNCLE

Milton Berle was a US comedian. He began his career at age ten in live singing performances. Later, he worked as a nightclub comedian and acted in films. In 1948, he took a role on *Texaco Star Theater,* a television variety show. The show was so popular some people bought their first television set just so they could watch it. Berle became known as "Uncle Miltie" and "Mr. Television."

CENSORSHIP

One of the first recorded moments of television censorship happened on May 25, 1944. NBC broadcast a show featuring radio star Eddie Cantor. Cantor sang a duet of "We're Having a Baby, My Baby and Me" with Nora Martin. The sound was cut off halfway through because the song was considered suggestive. When Cantor began dancing in a hula style, the cameraman was told to blur the picture by using soft focus. An NBC spokesman explained the decision: "The obligation of NBC to the public [is] to make certain that its facilities do not bring into American homes material which the audience would find objectionable."[6]

were often live. Any other shows had to be filmed and then the film was sent to the station. A film was typically made by pointing a camera at the video screen as the live show played. A show playing live in New York might show in a film version on another television station across the country weeks later.

As more stations started, television programming had to expand to meet this demand. Radio programs still provided the primary inspiration for television shows. The best options added visual appeal. In game shows, a handsome host led average Americans through humiliating but funny stunts. Variety acts, which featured different entertainers, dramatic series, and westerns also showed up on television.

Sports were also popular. In particular, boxing and wrestling showed up well on a small screen because the camera only had to focus on the boxing or wrestling ring. The *Gillette Cavalcade of Sports* debuted in 1944 and lasted 16 years. Razor company Gillette had been a longtime sponsor of radio programs. It was one of the first advertisers to commit to weekly television sponsorship, with three broadcasts a week.

Bigger, Better, More

By 1948, there were four networks, with a total of 52 stations in 29 cities. Nearly 1 million homes had television sets.[7] A much better television camera provided a sharper image. It also had a greater depth of field, so images both close and far away were in focus. This made it possible to capture an event taking place across a large stage or a large playing field. Television screens grew larger, approximately

Bad for You?

As television viewership increased, some people grew concerned about the power of television. By 1950, critics were accusing television of showing unnecessary sex and violence. Some people felt the violence in cop shows was a bad influence on children and blamed television for an increase in juvenile delinquency. Sex was not shown on television shows at the time, but protesters complained about comedians telling suggestive jokes and stories. They also criticized actresses wearing low-cut gowns. This sparked a national debate about proper attire for women in public. Most viewers, however, cared little about the controversies, as long as they were entertained.

seven to ten inches (18 to 25 cm) across the screen. A standard was set for 525 lines in the image. Television also took off in Europe after World War II. Each country had different standards. In the United Kingdom, television images were made up of 404 lines. The French used 819 lines.

By 1949, most major US cities had at least one television station and approximately 9 percent of homes had televisions. By 1952, half of all US homes had a television.[8] This increased the demand for programming and improving technology to transmit the programs.

Advances in technology helped connect television stations. A network of stations covered most of the East Coast and Midwest by 1949. By 1957, this network linked the entire country. A local station no longer had to provide all its programming. The four big networks provided shows for their local stations around the country without needing to mail films. Local stations could also provide their own content, such as local news.

Number of US Households

with Television 1950-2010

Year	Total US Households	Households with Television	Percent of Households with Television
1950	43,000,000	3,880,000	9.0
1955	47,620,000	30,700,000	64.5
1960	52,500,000	45,750,000	87.1
1965	56,900,000	52,700,000	92.6
1970	61,410,000	58,500,000	95.3
1975	70,520,000	68,500,000	97.1
1980	77,900,000	76,300,000	97.9
1985	86,530,000	84,900,000	98.1
1990	93,760,000	92,100,000	98.2
1995	97,060,000	95,400,000	98.3
2000	102,680,000	100,800,000	98.2
2005	111,630,000	109,600,000	98.2
2010	116,170,000	114,900,000	98.9[9]

The Golden Age of Television

Television didn't just learn from radio; it had a major effect on the competing medium. By the 1950s, as many people were watching television as were listening to radio in major cities. Radio was still earning money, while television networks were losing money, but people recognized the future lay with television. In order to cut costs, radio networks turned to musical shows, using a disc jockey and recorded music. The days of live radio performances, with variety shows, dramas, and comedies, were fading.

Television began replacing live theater, movies, and radio. After the war, the population shifted from cities to suburbs. There was also a baby boom as many couples

Bob Smith, with his puppet Howdy Doody, made *The Howdy Doody Show* one of the first successful children's television shows.

Television became a favorite leisure activity for many families after World War II.

started creating families. For these people, it was easier to stay home and watch television than go into the city for theater or movies.

One of the first children's television shows—and the most popular—was *The Howdy Doody Show*. It began in late 1947 as a spin-off from a radio program. Actor Bob Smith worked with marionette puppets. Live actors rounded out the cast. Crazy machines such as the

Honkadoodle, which translated Mother Goose's honks into English, played to the country's fascination with new technology.

The show was immediately successful and quickly extended to five days a week. Most early children's shows were mainly provided as a public service to educate children. *The Howdy Doody Show* included educational content balanced with laughs, and its popularity attracted major advertisers. Product messages were worked into songs and skits. Howdy Doody toys, records, and comic books were produced, bringing the popular television show into US homes even more. The show increased the popularity of television in general and showed it could be a moneymaker for advertisers and studios.

Funny Families

Before the rise of television, movies, and radio, vaudeville theater was the most popular form of entertainment. Vaudeville usually featured at least a dozen acts. These might include comedians, musicians, dancers, acrobats, jugglers, ventriloquists, animal trainers, and more. With the advent of movies, the vaudeville theater circuit faded. Radio provided an opportunity for some performers, but it did not provide visuals. Variety shows found a natural home on television.

Television executives brought the principles of vaudeville to television in a form called vaudeo. *The Ed Sullivan Show* began in 1948 and aired for 23 years. Ed Sullivan had been a sports reporter, gossip columnist, and radio host. Sullivan's live show balanced new talent with established stars. Classical artists, such as ballet dancers and opera singers, performed alongside groups such as singing firemen and jugglers. He introduced

Ed Sullivan, *center,* stands with the Beatles on the set of *The Ed Sullivan Show* in 1964.

rock 'n' roll to a wide audience, drawing in teenage viewers to bands such as the Beatles. At a time when viewers had few entertainment options, *The Ed Sullivan Show* had something for everyone.

Other shows continued drawing on formulas that came from radio. In the 1930s and 1940s, several comedies played on radio. These were sitcoms, or situation comedies, featuring average people with everyday problems. Some of these shows made the transition to television.

Everyone Loves *I Love Lucy*

One such sitcom was *I Love Lucy*. Comedian Lucille Ball had played in films and on a radio sitcom. She agreed to move her show to television if she could work in Hollywood, California, instead of New York. She also insisted her husband Desi Arnaz play her husband on television. The network was

COAST TO COAST

New York and California have a long history as rivals in the entertainment business. The movie industry had moved from New York to Hollywood in the early 1900s. Los Angeles gained most network radio programming in the late 1930s. At the beginning of television, most programs featured live performances, and New York was set up better for that. But around 1950, film techniques improved, and filmed television shows became better and cheaper. In addition, the cables laid across the country meant California production companies could send a high-quality picture to the East Coast. Hollywood soon took over much of the television business.

I Love Lucy

Lucille Ball and her husband Desi Arnaz put together *I Love Lucy* and insisted on starring in it together. They took a lower salary in exchange for full ownership rights.

I Love Lucy (1951–1957) was an instant hit due to Ball's outrageous comedic style and actions. The show featured Ball as a young housewife who wanted to do more, especially join her husband in show business. Her rebellions, from taking a job to trying to fool her husband, exposed the restrictions women faced in society. Her constant failures put her back in the home. Yet, Lucy never gave up trying to accomplish more, showing viewers the tension women faced at the time.

concerned viewers would not accept Arnaz, who was Cuban and had an accent. Ball and Arnaz toured in a nightclub act together to convince the studio they would be accepted.

The comedy was filmed rather than broadcast live. For most filmed television shows, shooting took place on a closed soundstage with one camera. *I Love Lucy* used three cameras and a studio audience to capture the energy of Ball's live performances. This technique became widely used in the 1970s.

I Love Lucy was the number one show in the country for four seasons. When Lucy had a baby in an episode, 72 percent of US homes with television tuned in.[1] Ball and Arnaz became the first millionaire television stars.

Reality Television

Reality television got its start early as well. *Candid Camera* premiered in 1948 and became the longest-running reality-based comedy program. It had already had some success as the radio show *Candid Microphone*. When asked about moving to television, host Allen Funt said he "wanted to go beyond what people merely said, to record what they did—their gestures, facial expressions, confusions, and delights."[2]

The format, featuring hoaxes caught on a hidden camera, seemed simple, but it provided many challenges. It took hours to prepare staged scenes, and many attempts failed. Microphones had to be concealed. Sometimes Funt wore a cast to hide one. Cameras were sometimes hidden behind screens. Bright lights were needed and had to be explained somehow, often as part of mock renovations. Network censors and sponsors had to approve each segment. Ultimately, only 10 percent of the filmed sequences could be used on the program.[3]

The show explored human psychology in ordinary contexts. In an era before home video recorders or YouTube, people were not used to seeing candid moments recorded. Funt said, "The audience saw ordinary people like themselves and the reality of events as they were unfolding."[4] The show revealed an audience appetite for watching real people in unscripted scenes. The show ran in various formats, on and off, until the year 2004. It inspired many other reality television shows.

Drama Television

Serious drama showed up on television as well. As the US population expanded and the economy grew, advertisers wanted to reach a more sophisticated audience than those who tuned in to game shows and variety acts. Dramas attracted this new audience, raised the status of television in general, and associated the television studio and the advertiser with a quality show. The first shows were fairly simple, filmed with two cameras in studios mainly in New York City. They lasted 30 to 60 minutes and borrowed elements from the theater, movies, and radio in a new format suitable for television. Many actors were movie actors and actresses. Camera angles and filming styles were also borrowed from cinema. Set designs and some acting techniques came from the theater, especially Broadway. As in radio, a narrator spoke after commercial breaks, providing continuity to the plot.

Drama shows were one reason the postwar years, from 1949 to roughly 1960, are sometimes considered the golden age of US television.

Well-known plays, such as works by William Shakespeare and Arthur Miller's *Death of a Salesman*, were produced for television. Both new popular literature and classics were adapted. However,

Hollywood film studios often bought the rights to popular works. The movie industry had a complicated relationship with television. Film studios viewed television as a rival medium and would not allow access to those works. This meant television studios had to look beyond already-existing material. Many of the shows produced were live, original dramas.

These drama programs performed a different play each week rather than an ongoing series with the same cast. That meant shows needed a steady supply of writers, actors, directors, and producers. Many actors got their starts in live television dramas. As television dramas won awards and praise, Broadway stage and Hollywood film stars became more willing to appear on television.

By 1955, dramas were a major part of network television schedules. Dramas often focused on a specific genre, such as mystery or suspense. Some programs were filmed rather than shown live. Live programming gave way to filmed shows in the last half of the 1950s. Film offered several advantages. Programs could be filmed outside a studio. Scenes could easily switch point of view or cut to close-ups. A show could move to a new location for each story—unless restrained by budget.

Filmed dramas introduced police, mystery, courtroom, and hospital series. By 1960, only one-third of all network programs were produced live.[5]

Despite the variety and creativity of dramas, the shows' producers were limited by advertiser demands. Many programs were sponsored by large US companies, such as Ford and Texaco. Most sponsors wanted shows to reflect middle-class values and avoid anything controversial. Scripts that explored social problems, such as racism and poverty, were rarely produced. But television would not be able to ignore social problems for long.

SPONSORS

Programs referenced their sponsors with names such as *Kraft Television Theatre, Ford Television Theatre, Goodyear Television Playhouse*, and *Texaco Star Theater*. The advertisers who paid for the shows chose the times they would play. In some cases, they regularly moved times and dates, searching for the best ratings. In 1953, the *Kraft Television Theatre* played twice on different networks. It showed on NBC on Wednesdays at 9:00 p.m. and on ABC on Thursdays at 9:30 p.m.

Chapter 5

Power of the Newsroom

*A*s television became a force in the United States, stations experimented with different news formats. *Meet the Press*, originally a radio program, moved to television in November 1947. It brought Washington politics to televisions across the nation and still airs today. At first, the show consisted of a panel of newspaper journalists interviewing a political newsmaker. Later, the show moved from a 30-minute program to one hour, with several interview segments and a roundtable discussion. Although the show rarely attracts a large audience, it has a strong effect on politics by holding candidates and elected officials accountable for their words and actions.

CBS offered live coverage of the entire March on Washington, including Martin Luther King Jr.'s speech, on August 28, 1963.

After World War II, a fear of communism swept the United States. Communism was seen as a threat to US interests at home and abroad. Communist governments had taken power in the Soviet Union after World War I and China after World War II. In 1950, North Korea, backed by the Soviet Union and China, invaded South Korea. The United States entered the Korean War on the side of South Korea.

Many Americans believed communism was a threat at home as well. Congress passed a security act requiring anyone affiliated with communism to submit to government supervision. Senator Joseph McCarthy of Wisconsin led a hunt for communists in the government. His aggressive tactics violated his suspects' civil rights, and many politicians, including President Dwight D. Eisenhower, disapproved. Still, his investigations led to 2,000 government employees losing their jobs, despite a lack of any proof of wrongdoing.[1] Then, McCarthy turned his attention to the military in a series of hearings in which he accused the army of blackmail and intimidation.

Using Television to Sway Opinions

The documentary news program *See It Now*, featuring journalist Edward R. Murrow, challenged McCarthy. On a March 9, 1954, show Murrow called for the public to oppose McCarthy. The Army-McCarthy hearings were broadcast on national television from April to June 1954. Americans could see McCarthy's intimidation tactics for themselves. His popularity vanished and his Senate colleagues expressed disapproval. These hearings proved how influential news television was on public opinion.

News took on a new format with the 1952 debut of *Today*, a morning news and talk show. It started as a two-hour program on weekdays. The show included coverage of national news, in-depth interviews with newsmakers, and local news updates. *Today*, also known as *The Today Show*, inspired similar shows in the United States and abroad. In early

SEE IT NOW

As television emerged as a force for news in the 1950s and 1960s, documentaries found a place on television. *See It Now* began airing in 1951. It pioneered techniques such as the use of live, unrehearsed interviews and original film clips. The show tackled many controversies. Producer Fred W. Friendly said, "TV is bigger than any story it reports. It's the greatest teaching tool since the printing press. It will determine nothing less than what kind of people we are."[2]

The original set of *Today* in New York City included a functional newsroom, bringing backstage activity on stage.

shows, the staff often walked through the newsroom set, and viewers could catch glimpses of camera crews and technicians. By 1955, the newsroom was hidden behind the scenes.

Covering the Civil Rights Movement

By the late 1950s, many Americans depended on television for their news. However, coverage of important events, such as the civil rights movement, was sporadic. The most violent events made the most impressive television spectacle, so they got the most coverage. Often a reporter spoke from the scene of the action. At other times, an anchor in the studio narrated events as they played on film. But the people actually participating in the events rarely had an opportunity to speak for themselves.

Television stations were still figuring out how to cover live events on August 28, 1963, when Dr. Martin Luther King Jr. led the March on Washington for Jobs and Freedom to promote civil rights. The commercial networks pooled their camera teams. Each station planned to broadcast live coverage throughout the day as they felt appropriate. No one was sure what would happen, and some people feared riots.

Instead of the expected 100,000 people, a crowd of 250,000 joined the march. Only CBS offered live coverage of the afternoon speeches. The other networks played their regular schedule of shows and offered edited recaps after the speeches. But they quickly realized

SATELLITE NEWS

Television news benefited from the use of communications satellites. Telstar, short for Telecommunications and Star, was designed to relay telephone, television, and telegraph messages. Bell Telephone Laboratories built the satellite and paid the National Aeronautics and Space Administration (NASA) to launch it. On July 11, 1962, one day after its launch, Telstar-1 transmitted the first television signals across the Atlantic Ocean. Other communication satellites followed. According to NASA, "The Americans had put into orbit a satellite that promised to tie together the ears and eyes of the world."[3]

viewers wanted to know more about the march. They scrambled to show more material. CBS produced an instant prime-time special. NBC played a rundown of the day's events instead of the first 45 minutes of the scheduled *The Tonight Show*.

Television began covering the civil rights movement more often. In 1964, civil rights leader Fannie Lou Hamer gave a speech on voting rights at the Democratic National Convention. An infuriated President Lyndon B. Johnson told the networks to kill the live feed of the speech. He offered an impromptu press conference instead. Yet, the networks recognized the importance of the speech and aired it later that night.

American Bandstand

American Bandstand began as a local television show in Philadelphia, Pennsylvania, and went nationwide in 1957. The show played popular music, while teenage studio guests offered opinions. Teenage regulars danced and showed off the latest fashions. In the early years, the show featured many African-American performers, but the studio rarely let African-American teens in. The producers may have been concerned about fights in a time of civil unrest as well as wanting to appeal to advertisers and white suburban viewers. Local African-American teenagers and parents protested. *American Bandstand* slowly integrated its dancers. However, only one African-American dancer performed on the show on August 28, 1963, the day of the March on Washington. By the 1970s, the show was more fully integrated.

Television also covered the 1964 murders of three civil rights workers. The victims were one African-American man from the South and two white men from the North. Several weeks of coverage taught people around the country about the deaths of the innocent volunteers. This helped convince white suburban viewers the civil rights movement could affect them. Televised images of the struggles—and the shocking violence—also helped build support for political changes.

President on Television

By the 1960s, politicians were aware of the power of television. Approximately 70 million viewers watched the first-ever televised presidential debate between Senator John F. Kennedy and Vice President Richard Nixon in 1960.[4] This was the first time most voters had been able to see the candidates in direct competition. Kennedy, who had been campaigning in California, was tan and rested. Nixon, who had recently spent two weeks in the hospital, was pale and underweight. Though experts thought the two did equally well in what they said, viewers praised the charismatic Kennedy. Producer and director Don Hewitt said, "When that debate was over, I realized that we didn't have to wait for an election day. We just elected a president. It all happened on television."[5] Since then, a strong television presence has been highly important for politicians in the United States and around the world.

President Kennedy embraced television in his short career. He invited television cameras to his first press conference. His wife, Jacqueline Kennedy, hosted a televised tour of the White House. In 1962, Kennedy requested airtime from all the broadcast networks. He had learned Cuba, aided by the Soviet Union, was building bases for nuclear missiles that could reach the United States. On television, Kennedy demanded the Soviets remove all missiles in Cuba. He warned the United States would take military action if the Soviets and Cuba did not comply.

Kennedy could have worked privately through diplomatic channels. By making his declaration

TELEVISION CAPTURES SPACE

Space missions shown on television often pulled in large audiences. The first astronauts became television celebrities. In the 1960s, every mission was a major media event. The biggest was the July 1969 *Apollo 11* mission. Hundreds of millions of people around the world watched the first lunar landing. They marveled at blurry, black-and-white images of Neil Armstrong jumping on the moon's surface. His statement "That's one small step for a man, one giant leap for mankind" symbolized the world coming together in wonder and hope.[6]

Television gave Kennedy an option for dealing with Cuba other than ordering air strikes and an invasion as his Joint Chiefs of Staff had recommended.

publicly in front of the entire country, it would be nearly impossible to back down. The crisis lasted 13 days, until the Soviets agreed to withdraw offensive weapons from Cuba. In return, the United States publicly declared it would not invade Cuba.

Kennedy dominated the airwaves again after his assassination on November 22, 1963. As the news came over wire services, television reporters scrambled to cover the story. News anchor Walter Cronkite

> **The instant replay premiered in 1963, repeating plays at real-time speed during an Army-Navy football game**

interrupted the soap opera *As the World Turns* with a voice-over announcement. Later, Cronkite appeared live on CBS, struggling with his emotions as he confirmed the death of the president. The tragedy preempted regular television programming for four days. Television coverage helped Americans process the news and start healing.

The public did not actually see the shooting on film, although a film existed. Time Life media company won a bidding war for the film and printed photos from it in *LIFE* magazine. The shooting was not played on television until 1975. However, when assassin Lee Harvey Oswald was shot by Jack Ruby on November 24, NBC broadcast the event live. CBS followed with a slow-motion replay of the shooting. Slow-motion replay was a new technology that had been used in sports coverage in the previous two years.

Soap Operas

In the early 1950s, CBS adapted several radio serials to television. In 1952, *Guiding Light* was the first radio soap opera to transition to television. Many television soaps followed the radio format of live, 15-minute episodes every weekday. Episodes were connected in an ongoing story, and Friday always ended on a cliffhanger moment. In 1956, *As the World Turns* aired as a 30-minute soap opera. With the additional time, the show featured more characters and explored more relationships, successfully phasing out the 15-minute soap opera.

By the late 1960s, soap operas were exploring serious cultural issues, such as ethnic and class differences, often in terms of romantic entanglements. *One Life to Live* sent a teenage drug addict to a treatment center. *All My Children*, which debuted in 1970, included the Vietnam War (1954–1975) in its stories.

Chapter 6

Diversity On-Screen

*W*hile the news covered civil rights, racial barriers broke down on television. African Americans usually played the roles of domestic help or were shown as comedic stereotypes. In the 1960s, more television shows included African-American characters as part of an integrated cast. These shows rarely touched on racial conflicts and did not challenge the standards of US culture. Instead, they showed African-American and Caucasian characters cooperating and living peacefully in an idealized world.

This new face of television allowed African-American actors to rise to stardom. Comedian Bill Cosby starred in *I Spy* from 1965 to 1968, earning

The Cosby Show aired from 1984 to 1992.

him three consecutive Emmys as Best Male Actor in a Dramatic Television Series. This success led to *The Bill Cosby Show* sitcom, which aired from 1969 to 1971. Cosby's multimillion-dollar contract with NBC included four variety specials. In an unusual move, the specials did not include major guest stars or acting skits but instead focused on Cosby's humorous stories.

Life as a Sitcom

By the 1970s, sitcoms regularly showed a variety of characters in challenging situations. Producer Norman Lear and director Alan "Bud" Yorkin led the way in combining comedy with serious and even controversial issues. Their well-known shows include

New Shows Fight for Viewers

Until the 1960s, networks had introduced new shows at any time from late September through mid-October. The thought was that viewers had a chance to check out new shows while still following their old favorites. A new show got its best start if it followed a proven hit. This favored the network with the most hit shows and made it hard for new shows to find an audience.

In 1963, ABC premiered all of its new shows in a single week, while the other networks were showing reruns. It did the same in 1964. The network, which had been third in the ratings, jumped to the number one spot. CBS and NBC fought back by scheduling their own season premieres all in one week. This began the system of television seasons and season premieres, which continues today.

All in the Family (1971–1983),
The Jeffersons (1975–1985),
and *Good Times* (1974–1979).

    All in the Family used
comedy to explore issues of
race, social inequality, and
sexuality. Television had
long-standing taboos against
profanity and racial slurs.
All in the Family shattered
those taboos. Much of
the drama came from
confrontations between conservative Archie, the main
character, and his liberal son-in-law. This set off a
national debate on whether comedy was an appropriate
forum for discussing prejudice and inequality. The
show also included belching and the sound of flushing
toilets, breaking another taboo against potty humor.
After a slow start, positive reviews and word of mouth
made the show the top-rated program on television.
The show won four Emmy Awards for Outstanding
Comedy Series.

    All in the Family also led to two spin-offs based
on African-American characters. The Bunkers'

In 1971, *All in the Family* became the first sitcom to feature a gay character. The first recurring gay character in prime time showed up on *The Corner Bar* the following year.

Isabel Sanford, *left*, Mike Evans, *top*, and Sherman Hemsley, *right*, pose as the Jefferson family.

African-American next-door neighbors got their own show as *The Jeffersons*. The title characters were millionaires living in a fancy Manhattan penthouse apartment. The show broke new ground by showing a wealthy African-American family. It also featured an interracial married couple as neighbors. Both shows used confrontational and ethnic humor. *The Jeffersons* received mixed reviews from African-American viewers. Some thought it was unrealistic and used negative stereotypes.

Good Times showed the harsh reality of life for many African Americans. It was a comedy, but it dealt with issues such as discrimination, unemployment, financial issues, mugging, and gang warfare. Both African Americans and Caucasians identified with many of the challenges the family faced.

Initially, *Good Times* portrayed good parenting, family unity, and courage in the face of diversity. Over time, the character of the teenage son J. J., played by Jimmie Walker, changed. He turned into a barely literate liar and thief with exaggerated comedic antics. This angered many in the African-American community. Esther Rolle and John Amos, who played the parents, left the show in protest. African Americans were finding new opportunities on television, but stereotypes had not disappeared.

ROOTS

Miniseries became popular in the 1970s. *Roots* was a 1977 miniseries that showed the experiences of several African-American generations as they went from slavery to freedom. This was one of the most watched miniseries of all time as it played over eight consecutive nights. According to *Publishers Weekly*, "*Roots* opened up the minds of Americans of all colors and faiths to one of the darkest and most painful parts of America's past."[1]

Working Women

Along with the portrayal of African Americans on television, the portrayal of women also changed in the 1970s. The 1960s had featured many lighthearted comedies. *Bewitched* (1964–1972) was a fantasy sitcom about a witch who was a suburban housewife. She often got her husband out of trouble, using either her magic or her creativity, but she always let him think he was successful on his own. The show lightly touched on a woman's role in marriage and society without challenging it.

Mary Tyler Moore was a famous television actress who got her big break starring as a wife and stay-at-home mother in *The Dick Van Dyke Show* (1961–1966). The show ended as the women's liberation movement,

A Television First

On November 1, 1972, *ABC Movie of the Week* on Wednesdays presented a made-for-television film called *That Certain Summer*. The movie tells the story of two men who become lovers. Both men are masculine, avoiding homosexual stereotypes. The story focuses on their personal struggles, particularly one man's attempt to explain his relationship to his teenage son. It was the first in-depth, sympathetic portrayal of homosexuality on US television. The program did very well in the ratings, proving at least some Americans were open to a concept that would have been taboo a few years before.

On *The Mary Tyler Moore Show*, an independent Moore interacted with coworkers, neighbors, friends, and dates.

a struggle for equality between the sexes, was starting. Moore went on to star in *The Mary Tyler Moore Show* (1970–1977), which featured a new brand of American woman: a single working woman. Showing a woman in her thirties focused on her career rather than a husband and children was a groundbreaking shift. Episodes dealt with issues such as equal pay, sexuality, and a woman's reputation. Other female characters helped portray a well-rounded picture of American women's lives. Television was reflecting real life, in which women had more choices.

Chapter 7

Power and Politics

*W*hile television series were tackling timely and controversial issues, television news started backing away from confrontation. Network news shows, such as *CBS News Hour* and *ABC Scope*, largely ignored political news stories or gave light coverage, biased toward the government. The number of hard news documentaries decreased in the late 1960s.

The best news was presented by public television. In contrast to the networks' commercial television, public television stations were less dependent on advertising income and had to promote the public good. Hundreds of independent local stations covered local and regional interests and educational programming.

News anchor Walter Cronkite, *center, with microphone*, helped bring Vietnam War news to US homes in the late 1960s.

Changing Perceptions of War

National Educational Television (NET), a noncommercial network, tackled serious issues. Shows covered misleading advertising and defects in US medical care. They exposed the ways supermarkets, phone companies, and credit unions unfairly charged the poor. They also probed into political misconduct.

In early 1967, the US Senate held hearings on the Vietnam War. NET covered the hearings. At first, ABC, CBS, and NBC largely ignored Vietnam War news and peace protests. They offered little coverage of the Senate hearings. They accepted the government's claim that the United States was winning the war. However, to catch up with NET, CBS sent a reporter to Vietnam to provide filmed reports. This reporting showed the strength of the United States' opponents. Either the US government was lying, or it was ignorant. People began questioning the United States' role in the war.

Before Vietnam, television had little effect on the public perception of war. The technology had either been nonexistent or in its infancy, with few viewers, during previous wars. That changed with Vietnam. Television brought the horrors of war to the US public. People saw US soldiers lighting village homes on fire and South Vietnamese planes accidentally killing their own fleeing civilians. Yet, most of the coverage was upbeat, focusing on the bravery and skill of US soldiers.

As the war dragged out, television journalists started expressing skepticism about the United States' ability to win the war. News reports focused on the human cost of the war. Reporters interviewed soldiers who considered the war senseless. At home, the antiwar movement was given more coverage. In 1968, popular news anchor Cronkite voiced his opinion, saying the war

FOR THE PUBLIC GOOD

NET was established in 1952 to help create and maintain television service focused on education. In 1967, the government created the Corporation for Public Broadcasting to establish standards and promote the development of public media. The government was supposed to supply funding to public television in the public interest. From the start, politicians haggled over how much money to provide. Still, this influx of money allowed public television to improve its shows. Boring lectures gave way to shows that were both informative and appealing. NET became the Public Broadcasting Service (PBS) in 1970.

was unwinnable. His thoughts reflected America's changing views of the war.

With faith in his leadership fading, President Johnson withdrew from the upcoming presidential campaign. Nixon, who had learned from his television debates against Kennedy in 1960, avoided requests for televised debates. Instead, he put together controlled press conferences with carefully chosen audiences.

News journalism can be dangerous. Many network personnel were wounded during the Vietnam War, and nine died.

Politicians and the Press at War

Once Nixon won the presidency in 1968, the balance of news coverage began shifting. The commercial networks began airing more controversial documentaries. But when they challenged Nixon's policies, he fought back. Aides leaked stories claiming network reports were false. The White House pressured the networks to cover a live speech by Vice President Spiro Agnew at a Republican Party conference. He claimed a select few people determined what played on the news.

He encouraged local stations to refuse to play network news programs. The networks continued producing news stories but endured pressure from the government, nervous local affiliates, and cautious advertisers.

Meanwhile, the Nixon administration also put pressure on public television. Making the president angry could result in a loss of government funding. In 1972, White House representative Clay T. Whitehead said, "There is a real question whether public television . . . should be carrying public affairs and news commentary, and that kind of thing."[2] Later that year, Nixon vetoed a spending bill that would have provided $155 million to public television over two years. Public television had no choice but to stop challenging White House policies.

Scandal

Both public and network television news programs were suffering from political pressure when a new scandal broke in June 1972. Burglars had broken into the Democratic

VETS ON SCREEN

The Vietnam War did not find much of a place in television fiction before it ended in 1975. In the next few years, Vietnam vets who appeared as minor characters in television shows were often shown as unstable. But in 1980, *Magnum, P.I.* premiered. The title character and his two closest friends were likable Vietnam vets. Soon other shows, such as *The A-Team, Riptide,* and *Airwolf,* featured veteran heroes.

National Committee's offices in the Watergate building in Washington, DC. Reporters for the *Washington Post* newspaper suggested a tie-in between the Nixon White House and the burglary. However, television and the public largely ignored the story.

In March 1973, the US Senate set up a committee to explore the accusations. The Nixon administration discouraged public television from offering live coverage. Some public stations rebelled and broadcast the event anyway. The commercial networks all covered the first week and then alternated coverage between the networks. Public interest grew, and ratings improved for news programs, despite the fact summer usually saw a drop in television viewership. Stations offered even more coverage. In the end, months of coverage resulted in no

Advertisement Bans

Health studies had emerged starting in 1939 linking cigarette smoking to higher rates of cancer and heart disease. In 1964, the Federal Trade Commission and the FCC declared advertisers had a responsibility to warn the public about the health risks of smoking. This led to warning labels on cigarettes and other regulation of the tobacco industry. At that time, tobacco companies were the largest product advertisers on television. On April 1, 1970, Nixon signed legislation banning cigarette advertisements on television and radio.

Americans watched Nixon resign on television
on August 8, 1974.

solid evidence of wrongdoing. However, many people
lost faith in the president.

The Nixon administration was rocked by more
scandals, and his attempts to improve his image on
television failed. In the summer of 1974, the House
Judiciary Committee began public impeachment
hearings. Television covered the debate and the voting.
Nixon resigned before a formal impeachment went
through. The networks canceled regular programming
and devoted four hours to the resignation and follow-up
analysis. Nixon would no longer manipulate the press.

New News Formats

With news back in a place of importance, the networks looked for ways to gain ratings. One option might have been to expand to a longer program. However, local stations wanted to save time for their own local newscasts. ABC tried broadcasting at 11:30 p.m., following the late local news. This meant going up against a very popular late-night talk show: *The Tonight Show Starring Johnny Carson*.

Late-night news got a boost in 1979 when Iranian militants took more than 50 US citizens hostage at the US Embassy in Iran. All the networks covered the crisis, but ABC had more time for in-depth coverage. People tuned in to *ABC News Nightline* to hear the updates and became accustomed to the late-night news program. *Nightline* remained on the air in 2014.

OLYMPIC TRAGEDY

The Olympics got only moderate television coverage in the 1960s. For the summer Olympics in 1972, ABC's *Wide World of Sports* offered extensive coverage in prime time and received high ratings. On September 5, the Olympics turned into a news story. A group of Palestinian terrorists had captured a group of Israeli athletes inside the Olympic compound. ABC provided daylong coverage of the hostage situation. That night, anchor Jim McKay shared the bad news with the United States. The hostages had all died in a shoot-out between the terrorists and police.

60 Minutes

Some news producers realized people wanted news with a human-interest angle, highlighting the personalities behind the stories. In 1968, CBS launched *60 Minutes*. The news show gave in-depth, 15-minute reports on national and international controversies. Reports focused on the characters involved, their motives, and the outcomes. After the Watergate scandal, show producers realized Americans might be interested in stories about criminal scams. Reports began exposing con men. In some cases, the show went undercover to expose a criminal. This brought up issues of journalistic integrity. Was it acceptable for a reporter to pose as someone else during a story? Was it unethical for the show to set up an operation to expose a crook?

At one point, *60 Minutes* turned the spotlight on themselves, asking journalists to address these questions. A reporter with *The Boston Globe* criticized the practices: "You're saying . . . that journalists have the right to use

60 MINUTES PROFITS

As it gained popularity, *60 Minutes* attracted advertisers and could charge more for advertisements, so it started turning a profit. Until that point, news programs had generally lost money. *60 Minutes* now offered prestige, high ratings, and income. News programs typically had a small budget compared to entertainment series, so a successful show was viewed as a bargain.

untruths, because we're going for the greater truth."[3] On the other hand, some journalists and most of the public believed it was good to catch the crooks in any way possible.

Another type of news program caught on during prime time. The news magazine format offered a mix of celebrity profiles, tips, and light feature stories. Throughout the 1980s, television news brought world events of all types to the public. More than 750 million people watched Prince Charles and Lady Diana wed in the United Kingdom in 1981.[4] When the Berlin Wall fell at the end of the decade, television was there. Television had truly allowed the American public to get to know its neighbors around the world.

The First Lady
of News

Barbara Walters joined *Today* as a writer in 1961. She worked on what were known as women's stories, such as fashion, and became a regular on-screen reporter in 1964. At first, she was not allowed to ask about so-called male topics, such as politics or economics, in her interviews. She conducted many well-received celebrity interviews and began targeting politicians as well. In 1974, she was named cohost on *Today*.

In 1976, Walters became coanchor of the *ABC Evening News*, the first woman to anchor a nightly newscast. Her male coanchor would not speak to her off the air. ABC reformatted the program as *World News Tonight*. The new show had no main anchor, but it featured Walters's exclusive interviews. She went on to interview every president and first lady who followed Nixon, along with many other important world leaders. The *New York Times* noted, "[Walters] remains the interviewer of record for American television."[5]

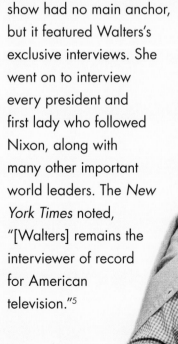

Chapter 8

Cable Television

*F*or decades, ABC, NBC, and CBS dominated television. The networks and their advertisers focused on shows that would appeal to as broad an audience as possible. CBS launched a trend of sitcoms dealing with current social issues. In 1975, ABC started focusing on kid-friendly programs. This often meant simple comedy or comedy combined with action or fantasy. The addition of sexually suggestive dialogue broadened the appeal to adults. By the late 1970s, ABC had moved further into sexually suggestive humor. All three networks also used violent action shows to draw in viewers. Despite minor differences, the networks offered similar fare and competed for the same audience.

In 1989, FOX's Bart Simpson and *The Simpsons* drew young
viewers with satire and humor.

Broadcast television networks, such as ABC, NBC, and CBS, create and distribute programming through local broadcast television stations. These stations often distribute local news shows in addition to national shows. Local stations use the public airwaves to broadcast the programming. Programs are free to households with television reception. They are also available through local cable, telephone, or satellite companies who deliver the programming to their customers. In contrast, a cable channel does not typically use public airwaves. Cable television was created in the 1940s to help reach areas where viewers were unable to receive public airwaves because of distance. Operators placed antennae in these areas to pick up signals from broadcast stations. These operators then used cables to distribute the signals and charged subscribers. Cable operators negotiate with the local cable, telephone, and satellite companies for distribution.

Television audiences started fragmenting with the growth of cable channels. The invention of the geostationary satellite allowed a local station to broadcast nationally or even globally. Home Box Office (HBO) hooked up to satellite in 1978 and began broadcasting nationwide. It also challenged traditional

Paying for HBO allows viewers to watch shows, such as *Game of Thrones*, without having to sit through commercials.

distribution methods by asking consumers to pay. This meant the network was not dependent on advertisers. Networks offered programs with no advertisements.

24-Hour Coverage

In 1980, media mogul Ted Turner founded the Cable News Network (CNN). CNN took advantage of the expanding cable industry. CNN was the first television station to offer 24-hour news coverage. The network struggled at first but gained respect and attention as it covered important events.

Other stations followed suit. Some identified their target audience in the station's name, such as Black Entertainment Television (BET) or The Christian Broadcasting Network (CBN). Many stations made additional money from advertising. Some also received fees from the local television stations that carried the

CNN continues to deliver the latest breaking news around the clock and around the world.

channels. However, since few people watched cable, budgets were low. In the beginning, most cable channels focused on old movies, reruns from network television, or sports. New programming included news, music videos, instructional shows, and religious sermons. For example, The Nashville Network (TNN) introduced inexpensive talent shows and travelogues, or travel documentaries. By 1985, almost one-half of the homes in the United States subscribed to cable.[1]

New Networks

FOX Broadcasting Company debuted in 1986 as a new, fourth network. At first, the station broadcast for only two hours on Sunday nights, but two FOX shows during that time slot established the FOX identity. *Married . . . with Children* (1987–1997) offered an alternative to the family-friendly sitcom, with a dysfunctional family and raunchy humor. *The Tracey Ullman Show* (1987–1990) was a high-quality variety show that brought FOX an Emmy nomination. The show also introduced the Simpson family as short animations shown between Ullman's skits. Soon getting its own show, *The Simpsons* (1989–) showcases a dysfunctional family that satirizes US life and popular culture. These shows gave FOX a hold on the important age 18 to 34 demographic.

It took until 1993 for FOX to broadcast seven nights a week. By then, it had introduced a number of reality shows, which earned high ratings at a low expense. One-hour dramas set at high schools, such as *21 Jump Street* (1987–1990) and *Beverly Hills, 90210* (1990–2000), helped bring in a teen audience.

Two more new networks debuted in 1995: the United Paramount Network (UPN) and Warner Bros. (WB). These networks brought Hollywood and television together. UPN built on its *Star Trek* franchise, while WB drew on the Warner Bros. movie and cartoon library. By that time, cable had become a big business. Cable companies started offering bundles of shows and charging viewers high monthly fees. The fees are paid to different channels depending on their popularity. In the bundled

SEX AND VIOLENCE

Politicians, media scholars, and behavioral scientists have debated the impact of television, especially on children. With the growth of cable channels and looser social standards, more sex, violence, and profanity appeared on television. In 1989, a suburban mother began a letter-writing campaign to advertisers of *Married . . . with Children.* She accused them of "helping to feed our kids a steady diet of gratuitous sex and violence."[2] Some businesses temporarily pulled their advertisements. However, the publicity brought the show more viewers, drawing in more advertisers.

system, cable subscribers pay these fees regardless of whether they watch a particular channel.

More Choices

Meanwhile, cable networks, such as Showtime and HBO, started airing more original programming. This was a way for them to create a clear brand identity. Nickelodeon used child-oriented sitcoms to establish itself as a station for children. Music channel Music Television (MTV) targeted teenagers with game shows, talk shows, cartoons, and reality programming, all heavy on the latest music and pop cultural references.

Minority groups started finding more options. NBC presented Bill Cosby's latest sitcom, *The Cosby Show* (1984–1992), and *The Fresh Prince of Bel-Air* (1990–1996), focusing on suburban, upper middle-class African Americans. FOX introduced shows targeting urban, lower- and middle-class African Americans, with shows such as *In Living Color* (1990–1994), *Martin* (1992–1997), and *The Sinbad Show* (1993–1994).

In 2013, ESPN was the most profitable channel, receiving $5.54 a month per customer, while CNN received sixty cents and the Hallmark Channel received six cents each month.[3]

FOX started dropping African-American programs in the late 1990s, and UPN took over. WB began targeting teenage girls and young women with shows such as *Buffy the Vampire Slayer* (1997–2002). Hispanics had little presence on network television, but cable stations such as Telemundo and Univision broadcast to them. By targeting a particular age and ethnic group, new stations could find an audience. Advertisers wanting to reach a specific audience paid well, even if the number of viewers was not large.

Freedom in Cable

Cable stations could focus on a narrow audience rather than trying to appeal to a large, general audience of middle-class families. Plus, many were ad-free,

Oprah's Rise

Oprah Winfrey began her television career as a local news anchor. In early 1984, she took over as host for *A.M. Chicago*. The show quickly moved from last place to first place in the ratings. *The Oprah Winfrey Show* launched with national distribution in 1986. The show focused on everyday people, with interviews, self-improvement advice, and book clubs. Winfrey has said that as an admired African-American woman with power and influence, she could make a positive difference in people's lives. *The Oprah Winfrey Show* ran for 25 seasons until 2011. It won 47 Daytime Emmy Awards. Winfrey also acted in movies and launched the Oprah Winfrey Network (OWN) on cable.

meaning they did not have to please advertisers worried about boycotts. This freedom meant cable shows often used more explicit language, sexuality, and violence than the traditional networks. They also tackled controversial subjects such as the AIDS epidemic, abortion, and child abuse in made-for-television movies.

In 2001, the average US household received 55 television channels.[4] With so many choices, fewer people watched each show. Yet, this fragmented market actually offered more opportunities for high-quality television. HBO began producing original, high-quality dramas. These shows did not have to appeal to a mass audience. They did have to appeal to people willing to pay the cable channel's subscriber fee.

LOOSER STANDARDS

For decades, alcohol makers advertised only beer and wine on television, not hard liquor. This was a voluntary ban, designed to reduce children's exposure to drinks with higher alcohol content. Cable networks began carrying advertisements for hard liquor in the mid-1990s. Young people were exposed to 30 times the number of liquor advertisements in 2009 as they were in 2001.[5] Lawmakers, medical groups, and the public opposed liquor advertisements on network television. However, in recent years, liquor companies have begun advertising hard alcohol on late-night network television. On cable, alcohol may be advertised at any time.

Getting Real

HILL STREET BLUES

The NBC show *Hill Street Blues* (1981–1987) was essentially a cop show blended with a soap opera. The show transformed the television drama. The dialogue was highly literate and story lines were not always comfortably resolved. The show borrowed from documentary cinema with a realistic style. The camera cut quickly between multiple story lines and had a large ensemble cast. The show inspired many quality dramas.

The growth of broadcast networks and cable stations means thousands of shows are needed every week. Not every show can be a big-budget extravaganza. And not every viewer wants only sophisticated scripted shows. In 1988, television writers went on strike for five months. Producers began looking for options that would not require writers. This led to the show *COPS*, a reality series following law enforcement at work. In 1992, MTV debuted *The Real World*, a show in which cameras followed several young people sharing a house. Viewers seemed fascinated by the tensions that arose from conflicting personalities.

The reality genre that had started with *Candid Camera* in 1948 exploded with many variations. *Survivor* (2000–) brought in a game show element, as groups of strangers competed for a cash prize. Celebrities offered a peek into their lives in shows such as *The Osbournes*

(2002–2005). *American Idol* (2002–) brought back the talent show. Both people and homes got makeovers on *Extreme Makeover* (2002–2007) and *Extreme Makeover: Home Edition* (2008–2009). Shows such as *Ice Road Truckers* (2007–) and *Dirty Jobs* (2005–2012) showed how other people live.

One of the biggest advantages to reality television is cheaper production prices. There are fewer paid performers, simpler sets, and less equipment. In 2014, a reality program typically costs less than $500,000 for an hour, which is roughly one-third the cost of a comedy or drama.[6] Product placements within the show can bring in additional money. In using product placement, manufacturers pay for their goods to be featured in movies and television programs. By the new millennium, television offered something for almost everyone.

The "Untalent" Show

The Gong Show (1976–1980, 1988) was a talent show with a difference. Instead of showcasing known talents, amateur performers had at least 45 seconds to showcase their acts. A panel of three celebrity judges could end the performance quickly by banging on a gong. Acts that didn't get gonged were ranked by the judges. The winner got $516.32. *The Gong Show* was a precursor to shows such as *America's Got Talent* and the audition episodes of *American Idol.*

Chapter 9

Global Media

Television is by no means an exclusive US entertainment form. By 1958, 26 countries had commercial television.[1] Most countries had a national television service to provide local and national news. Some produced original programming, but it was cheaper to buy US television series. US networks developed a presence in many countries, from Argentina and Australia to Venezuela and Yugoslavia. Selling US television series abroad provided income for the major networks.

Satellite technology provided an even greater reach for US shows. *Baywatch* (1989–2001), a show about lifeguards in California, was viewed in 148 countries

ABC's *Modern Family*, featuring Ty Burrell, *right*, and Julie Bowen, *left*, is a popular sitcom viewed by millions around the world.

and 44 languages, reaching more than 1 billion adult viewers worldwide.[2] The show played well to international audiences because it focused on attractive characters in action sequences, instead of complicated plots and dialogue. Complicated plots and extensive dialogue are harder to translate.

Streaming

The Internet has provided an even greater reach for new and old shows. Most shows are not available online when they first broadcast, but the Internet is a great publicity tool regardless. Networks provide their schedules online. Popular shows may have official websites or unofficial fan web pages. Bulletin boards or chat rooms allow viewers to discuss the show. In the past, it

Chinese Cable Television

Some countries grew concerned about the influence of US television on their local culture. In 1993, China prohibited citizens from using satellite television dishes. The country also pushed forward development of its own state-run cable systems. By 1996, Chinese cable television had 40 million subscribers.[3] China also formed its own satellite channels with Chinese opera, sports, and films. Once it was able to offer this local competition, China allowed international satellite television as well. China Central Television also attempted to attract viewers who were interested in foreigners. Several shows featured Chinese immigrants in the United States or Americans and Europeans in China.

might have taken months or years for a fan community to develop and for fans to find each other. The Internet provides instant connections.

While the Internet helps promote television shows, not all networks are in complete favor of the Internet. People may post spoilers about episodes that have not yet played in some countries. Television production has gotten more secretive in order to protect the surprises. Some networks have shut down unofficial fan sites they believed infringed on their copyrights. The Internet can also enable pirates to share programs illegally.

The growth of high-speed Internet after 2000 brought even more options for viewers. Some services offered shows for free, with advertising. In 2006, AOL's In2TV and CBS Innertube both launched under this model, mainly offering shows that had already played on network television. In 2008, NBCUniversal launched Hulu, which offered movies and television series from NBC, FOX, Disney, and other companies. On the other hand, Netflix, a streaming on-demand company, charges consumers a monthly fee. Netflix pays network and cable stations millions of dollars for access to their shows.

Streaming services also offer their own original programming. Netflix has a $3 billion budget for new programs. It began offering Netflix original shows in 2012, starting with *Lilyhammer* in 2012 and *House of Cards* in 2013. Netflix sees original programming as a way to draw in more subscribers.

Online superstore Amazon has also started offering original programming for its instant video-streaming service called Amazon Prime. Amazon hopes to keep members of its Prime shipping service by offering more perks. This may affect how much cable companies are able to charge for cable bundles and even whether network television survives in its current form.

Endless Choices

In the new millennium, hundreds of cable stations, plus access to television shows through streaming video, mean endless choices. People can no longer assume their neighbors, classmates, and coworkers have all seen the same shows. Small communities of fans may develop, especially through social media, but television no longer connects the country the way it once did. Yet, some breakout shows still get the whole country talking.

Breaking Bad (2008–2013) was an unlikely drama about a high school chemistry teacher with cancer who decides to earn money by dealing drugs. Critics called the show one of the best television dramas ever. Only 1.4 million viewers watched the debut of *Breaking Bad*.[5] That seems low compared to the 44 million who watched Lucy give birth on *I Love Lucy* in 1953.[6] But buzz built over time, and many people caught up on the show by watching it on Netflix or iTunes. Having access to an entire season through streaming allowed viewers to watch multiple episodes back-to-back. By the final episode, 10.3 million viewers tuned in for the broadcast.[7] Even more watched it later, and many people who never watched an episode heard about the show.

BREAKING BAD BENEFITS FROM STREAMING

After *Breaking Bad* won an Emmy for Best Drama, creator Vince Gilligan said, "I think Netflix kept us over here. . . . I don't think our show would have even lasted beyond season two if not for streaming video on demand, and also the social Internet component of it, where folks get to chat online with folks all around the world afterward really has helped. It's a golden era of television, and we've been really fortunate that we've reaped the benefits of these two wonderful developments."[8]

When people stream or record shows to watch later on their computers or mobile devices, they can skip advertising. This cuts into the profits the network can make from advertisements. Network television is finding ways to get people to turn on the television and watch a program as it broadcasts. Live events are perfect for this. Sports, which are often broadcast live, draw in an audience that does not want to risk hearing the results before they see the game. Award shows, such as the Oscars, also offer a must-see-it-now experience. Social media supports these shows as people share their reactions on Twitter or Facebook during the event. Other live programs offer fashion advice, comedy, or talk shows. The medium that started with live shows out of necessity is revisiting the concept for marketing.

People have many choices for entertainment, but television is successfully fighting for market share. The history of television has passed in the blink of an eye compared to other art forms, such as music and dance. Yet, in less than a century, television has changed dramatically, and it has changed US culture with it. Television shares news from around the world, affecting how people think and live. It brings people together in discussions about popular shows or major sporting

Worldwide Mobile
Streaming Projected to Rise

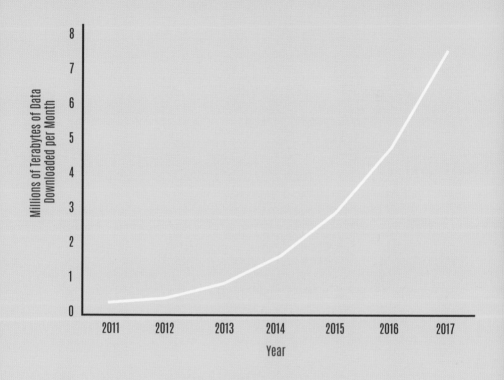

events. It teaches people about diverse cultures both at home and abroad. It provides advice and instruction on everything from cooking gourmet meals to handling relationships. Television, once a uniting force in the United States, now allows and encourages individuality.

TIMELINE

1906

The first radio program of speech and music is transmitted to the public.

1920

The first commercial radio stations open.

1926

On January 27, the first television is demonstrated in the United Kingdom.

1927

On September 7, Philo T. Farnsworth demonstrates the electronic transmission of television to his financial backers.

1927

Congress signs off on the establishment of the Federal Radio Commission (FRC) to regulate the airwaves in America.

1939

NBC demonstrates television service at the New York World's Fair.

1941

The FCC approves commercial television in May.

1945

NBC splits into two companies, creating the American Broadcasting Company (ABC).

1948

Nearly 1 million American homes have television sets.

1949

Most major US cities have at least one television station. A network of cable and microwave links connect television stations across most of the East Coast and Midwest.

1952

Half of all US homes own a television.

TIMELINE CONTINUED

1954
The first color television sets are sold.

1962
In October, the networks cover President John F. Kennedy's speech about the Cuban missile crisis.

1967
The government creates the Corporation for Public Broadcasting to establish standards and to promote the development of public media.

1970
On April 1, President Richard Nixon signs legislation banning cigarette advertisements on television and radio.

1972
On November 1, *ABC Movie of the Week* presents *That Certain Summer*, a sympathetic portrayal of homosexuality.

1974
Television covers the House Judiciary Committee impeachment hearings for Nixon.

1976
Barbara Walters becomes the first woman to anchor a nightly newscast.

1978
HBO hooks up to satellite and begins broadcasting nationwide.

1980
The Cable News Network (CNN) debuts.

1986
FOX Broadcasting Company becomes the fourth network.

2012
Netflix begins offering original television shows, while continuing to offer movies.

GLOSSARY

boycott
To refuse to buy or use a product as a means of influencing the manufacturer.

broadcast
A radio or television program or transmission.

censorship
The practice of examining material such as news or entertainment and removing anything considered unacceptable.

communism
Political theory promoting a society in which all property is publicly owned.

frequency
The rate at which a vibration occurs to make up a wave, as in sound, radio, or light waves.

geostationary satellite
A satellite that travels above the earth's equator at the same speed as the earth rotates, so the satellite always remains in the same spot above the earth.

hard news
Serious, important news concerning topics such as politics and world events.

impeachment
A process in which an official is accused of unlawful activity that may result in the official being removed from office.

newsreel
A short film of news and current events.

patent

An official document that gives a person or company the right to be the only one that makes or sells a product.

prime time

The time at which the greatest number of people are expected to be watching television, usually between 8:00 p.m. and 11:00 p.m.

royalty

Money paid to a creator based on how many copies have been sold.

satellite

An artificial body placed in orbit for communication or to collect information.

sponsor

A person or organization, such as an advertiser, that provides money for a project.

taboo

Not socially acceptable.

transmit

To broadcast or send out a radio or television program.

ADDITIONAL RESOURCES

Selected Bibliography

Castleman, Harry, and Walter J. Podrazik. *Watching TV: Six Decades of American Television*. Syracuse, NY: Syracuse UP, 2010. Print.

Hilmes, Michele, ed. *The Television History Book*. London: British Film Institute, 2003. Print.

Further Readings

Krull, Kathleen. *The Boy Who Invented TV: The Story of Philo Farnsworth*. New York: Dragonfly, 2014. Print.

Nardo, Don. *The History of Television*. Farmington Hills, MI: Lucent, 2009. Print.

Sandler, Martin W. *Kennedy through the Lens: How Photography and Television Revealed and Shaped an Extraordinary Leader*. London: Walker Children's, 2011. Print.

Websites

To learn more about Essential Library of Cultural History, visit **booklinks.abdopublishing.com**. These links are routinely monitored and updated to provide the most current information available.

Places to Visit

Early Television Foundation and Museum
5396 Franklin Street
Hilliard, Ohio 43026
614-771-0510
http://www.earlytelevision.org
View and purchase a wide collection of television artifacts.

Museum of Broadcast Communications
360 North State Street
Chicago, IL 60654
312-245-8200
http://www.museum.tv/index.htm
Walk through the museum to see television screenings, exhibits, and studios.

SOURCE NOTES

Chapter 1. Television Connects Cultures

1. David Bauder. "Nielsen Study Reveals How TV Viewing Is Changing." *HUFFPOST TV*. Huffington Post, 9 Nov. 2012. Web. 29 July 2014.

2. Ibid.

Chapter 2. Radio with Pictures

1. "A Short History of Radio: With an Inside Focus on Mobile Radio." *FCC*. Federal Communications Commission, n.d. Web. 2 June 2014.

2. "Mechanical Television." *Early Television Museum*. Early Television Museum, n.d. Web. 2 June 2014.

3. Harry Castleman and Walter J. Podrazik. *Watching TV: Six Decades of American Television*. Syracuse, NY: Syracuse UP, 2010. Print. 2–3.

4. "Big Dream, Small Screen Transcript." *American Experience*. Corporation for Public Broadcasting, n.d. Web. 2 June 2014.

Chapter 3. Rise and Fall and Rise Again

1. "Big Dream, Small Screen Transcript." *American Experience*. Corporation for Public Broadcasting, n.d. Web. 2 June 2014.

2. Diane Petro. "Brother, Can You Spare a Dime?: The 1940 Census: Employment and Income." *Prologue Magazine*. US National Archives and Records Administration, 2012. Web. 11 June 2014.

3. Harry Castleman and Walter J. Podrazik. *Watching TV: Six Decades of American Television*. Syracuse, NY: Syracuse UP, 2010. Print. 110–114.

4. "Golden Age, 1930s through 1950s." *FCC*. Federal Communications Commission, n.d. Web. 4 June 2014.

5. Ibid.

6. Michele Hilmes and Jason Jacobs, eds. *The Television History Book*. London: British Film Institute, 2003. Print. 10.

7. "Postwar American Television: Estimated US TV Sets and Stations." *Early Television Museum*. Early Television Museum, n.d. Web. 5 June 2014.

8. "Television's First Act of Censorship." *Television Obscurities*. Television Obscurities, 25 July 2009. Web. 4 June 2014.

9. "TV Basics." *TVB.org*. TVB Local Media Marketing Solutions, June 2012. Web. 4 June 2014.

Chapter 4. The Golden Age of Television

1. Christopher Anderson. "I Love Lucy." *Archive of American Television*. Academy of Television Arts & Sciences Foundation, n.d. Web. 5 June 2014.

2. Amy Loomis. "Candid Camera." *Archive of American Television*. Academy of Television Arts & Sciences Foundation, n.d. Web. 5 June 2014.

3. Ibid.

4. Ibid.

5. "A Brief History of Television." *Archive of American Television*. Academy of Television Arts & Sciences Foundation, n.d. Web. 5 June 2014.

Chapter 5. Power of the Newsroom

1. "Joseph R. McCarthy." *History.com*. A&E Television Networks, LLC, n.d. Web. 11 June 2014.

2. Eric Page. "Fred W. Friendly, CBS Executive and Pioneer in TV News Coverage, Dies at 82." *New York Times*. New York Times, 5 Mar. 1998. Web. 11 June 2014.

3. Elizabeth Howell. "Telstar: Satellites Beamed 1st TV Signals Across the Sea." *SPACE.com*. Purch, 12 Feb. 2013. Web. 11 June 2014.

4. Erika Tyner Allen. "Kennedy–Nixon Debates." *Archive of American Television*. Academy of Television Arts & Sciences Foundation, n.d. Web. 5 June 2014.

5. Ibid.

6. Chris Paterson. "Moon Landing." *Archive of American Television*. Academy of Television Arts & Sciences Foundation, n.d. Web. 5 June 2014.

Chapter 6. Diversity On-Screen

1. "Miniseries: Roots Special." *TPT*. Public Broadcasting Service, n.d. Web. 13 June 2014.

SOURCE NOTES CONTINUED

Chapter 7. Power and Politics

1. Harry Castleman and Walter J. Podrazik. *Watching TV: Six Decades of American Television*. Syracuse, NY: Syracuse UP, 2010. Print. 184.

2. Ibid. 229.

3. Ian Jackman, ed. *Con Men*. New York: Simon & Schuster, 2003. Print. xi–xiv.

4. Jennie Wood. "How Prince Charles and Diana's 1981 Royal Wedding Compares." *Infoplease*. Pearson Education, 2007. Web. 12 June 2014.

5. "Barbara Walters." *The Paley Center for Media*. The Paley Center for Media, n.d. Web. 15 June 2014.

Chapter 8. Cable Television

1. Michele Hilmes. *The Television History Book*. London: British Film Institute, 2003. Print. 63–64.

2. Ibid. 110.

3. Dan Bobkoff. "The History—And Future—Of Cable's Bundling." *NPR*. NPR, 7 Aug. 2013. Web. 28 July 2014.

4. Michele Hilmes. *The Television History Book*. London: British Film Institute, 2003. Print. 64.

5. Mike Esterl. "Liquor Ads Win Airtime." *Wall Street Journal*. Wall Street Journal, 23 Aug. 2012. Web. 17 June 2014.

6. Charles B. Slocum. "The Real History of Reality TV." *WGAW*. Writers Guild of America, West, n.d. Web. 18 June 2014.

Chapter 9. Global Media

1. Michele Hilmes. *The Television History Book*. London: British Film Institute, 2003. Print. 115.

2. Ibid. 117.

3. Ibid. 116.

4. Ilan Mochari. "The History of Netflix and the Future of Television." *Inc*. Inc., 30 Jan. 2014. Web. 18 June 2014.

5. James Hibberd. "'Breaking Bad' Series Finale Ratings Smash All Records." *Entertainment Weekly*. Entertainment Weekly and Time Inc., 30 Sept. 2013. Web. 18 June 2014.

6. Sofia M. Fernandez. "'I Love Lucy': 5 Things to Know about the Series." *The Hollywood Reporter*. The Hollywood Reporter, 6 Aug. 2011. Web. 20 June 2014.

7. James Hibberd. "'Breaking Bad' Series Finale Ratings Smash All Records." *Entertainment Weekly*. Entertainment Weekly and Time Inc., 30 Sept. 2013. Web. 18 June 2014.

8. Katie Atkinson. "'Breaking Bad' Wouldn't Exist without Netflix, Creator Says after Emmy Win." *Entertainment Weekly*. Entertainment Weekly and Time Inc., 23 Sept. 2013. Web. 19 June 2014.

INDEX

111

ABOUT THE AUTHOR

Chris Eboch, aka M. M. Eboch, writes about science, history, and culture for all ages. Her novels for young people include historical fiction, ghost stories, and action-packed adventures.